THE MOST REQUESTED
Broadway Songs

Cherry Lane Music Company
Director of Publications: Mark Phillips

ISBN 978-1-4584-0988-1

Visit our website at www.cherrylaneprint.com

CONTENTS

All I Ask of You

from THE PHANTOM OF THE OPERA

Lyrics by Charles Hart
Additional Lyrics by Richard Stilgoe

Music by Andrew Lloyd Webber

Andante

RAOUL:

No more talk of dark-ness, for-get these wide-eyed fears: I'm

here, noth-ing can harm you, my words will warm and calm you.

Let me be your free-dom, let day-light dry your tears: I'm

here, with you, be-side you, to guard you and to guide you.

CHRISTINE:
Say you love me ev-ery wak-ing mo-ment, turn my head with talk of

sum-mer-time. Say you need me with you now and al-ways;

prom-ise me that all you say is true, that's all I ask of

And I Am Telling You I'm Not Going

from DREAMGIRLS

Lyric by Tom Eyen

Music by Henry Krieger

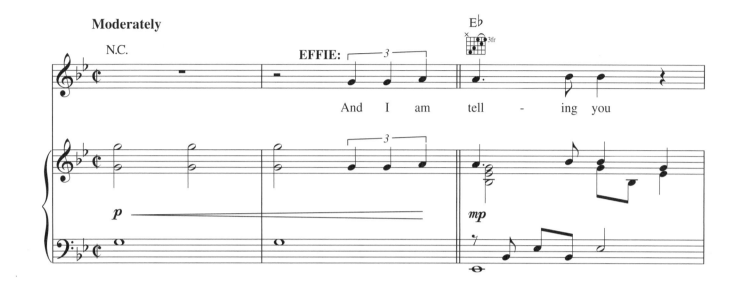

liv - in' with - out you. ___ I'm not liv - in' with - out ___ you.

You see, there's just no way, there's no ___ way. ___

Funky

Tear down the moun - tains, yell, ___ scream and shout. You can

say what you want, ___ I'm not walk - in' out. Stop all the riv - ers, push, ___

14

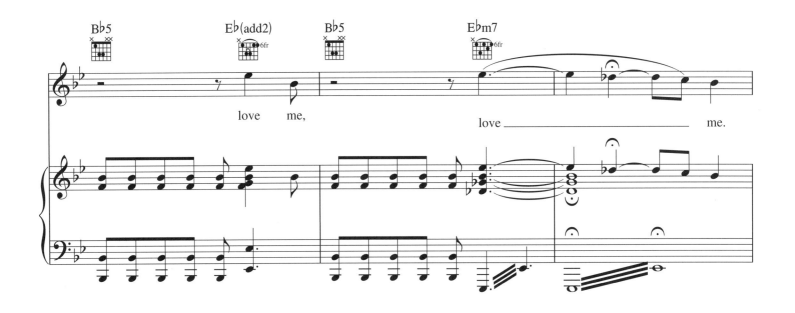

love me, love _____ me.

Freely

You're gon - na love _____

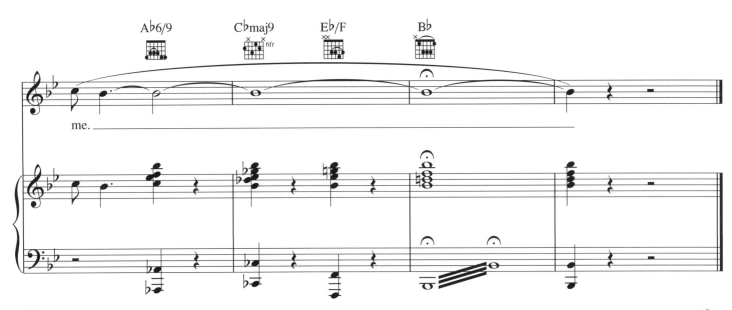

me. _____

Be Our Guest

from Walt Disney's BEAUTY AND THE BEAST: THE BROADWAY MUSICAL

Lyrics by Howard Ashman

Music by Alan Menken

LUMIERE: *Ma chère Mademoiselle! It is with deepest pride and greatest pleasure that*

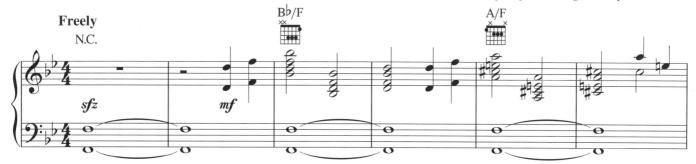

we welcome you here tonight. And now, we invite you to relax. Let us pull up a chair as the dining room proudly presents...

chest.   Let   us   say   for   your *en* - *trée* we've   an   ar -

ray.   May   we   sug - gest: try   the   bread!   Try   the   soup!   When   the

crou - tons   loop   de   loop **WOMEN:** it's   a   treat   for   an - y

din - er.   Don't   be - lieve   me?   Ask   the   chi - na.   Sing - ing **MEN:**

pork! Danc - ing veal! What an en - ter - tain - ing

meal! **ALL:** How could an - y - one be gloom - y or de -

pressed? _____ We'll make you shout "en - core" ____ and send us

out for more. _____ So, be our guest! Be our

guest! Be our guest! _____

Ah

G7sus

joyfully

G7

MRS. POTTS: It's a

_mp_

C   Cmaj7   C6   C

guest!   It's   a   guest!   Sakes a - live,   well,   I'll   be   blessed.   Wine's   been

poured and, thank the Lord, I've had the nap-kins fresh-ly pressed. With des-

sert she'll want tea. And, my dear, that's fine with me. While the

cups do their soft - shoe-ing, I'll be bub-bling, I'll be brew-ing. I'll get

warm pip-ing hot. Heav-en's sake, is that a spot? Clean it up!_

Fast 2, Broadway style

here   and   we're   ob - sessed! _____   With   your

meal,   with   your   ease,   yes   in -

deed,   we   aim   to   please.   While   the

can - dle - light's   still   glow - ing,   let   us

Much slower

A tempo

Beauty and the Beast

from Walt Disney's BEAUTY AND THE BEAST: THE BROADWAY MUSICAL

Lyrics by Howard Ashman

Music by Alan Menken

Being Alive

from COMPANY

Music and Lyrics by
Stephen Sondheim

Moderato (♩=112)

ROBERT:

Some - one to hold you too close,
Some - one to need you too much,

Some - one to hurt you too deep,
Some - one to know you too well,

Some - one to sit in your chair,
Some - one to pull you up short,

To ru - in your sleep,
to put you through hell,

to make you a - ware
and give you sup - port

Of be - ing a - live,
Is be - ing a - live,

loco

* *Add notes in parentheses 2nd time only.*

8vb

Be - ing a - live. _____ live, _____ Be - ing a - live. _____

2nd time
cresc. poco a poco

(*cresc. poco a poco*)

Some - one you have to let in,

p *sub.*

Some - one whose feel - ings you spare, Some - one who, like it or

not, Will want you to share A lit-tle a lot, is be-ing a-

live, _____ Be - ing a - live. _____

Some - one to crowd you with love,

Some - one to force you to care, Some - one to make you come

Add notes in parentheses 2nd time only.

sleep and make me a - ware Of be - ing a - live,
hell and give me sup - port For be - ing a - live,

1

Be - ing a - live.
Make me a -

2nd time
cresc. poco a poco

2

live,

Make me a -

live.

Make me con -

live.

Some - bod - y crowd me with love,

Some - bod - y force me to care. Some - bod - y let me come

through, I'll al - ways be there as fright - ened as you, To help us sur -

Bewitched

from PAL JOEY

Words by Lorenz Hart

Music by Richard Rodgers

He's a fool and don't I know it, But a fool can have his charms;

I'm in love and don't I show it, Like a babe in arms.

Love's the same old sad sen - sa - tion, Late - ly I've not slept a wink,

Broadway Baby

from FOLLIES

Music and Lyrics by
Stephen Sondheim

Broad-way ba-by,_____ Learn - ing how to sing and dance,

Wait-ing for that one big chance_____ To be in a show._____

Gee,____ I'd like to__ be_____ on some mar - quee,_____ All__ twin -

kl - ing lights,__ A spark__ To pierce the__ dark_____ From Bat - t'ry__ Park__

To Wash - ing-ton Heights. Some day, may-be,

All my dreams will be re-paid. Hell, I'd ev-en play the maid

To be in a show.

Say, Mis - ter Pro-du - cer, Some girls get the breaks.

Just give me my cue, sir. I've got what it takes.

Say, Mis - ter Pro - du - cer, I'm talk - in' to you,

— sir: I don't need a lot, On - ly what I got,

Plus a tube of grease - paint And a fol - low spot! I'm a

Broad-way ba-by,_____ Slav-ing at a five-and-ten,_____

Dream-ing of the great day when_____ I'll be in a

show._____

Broad-way ba-by,_____ Mak-ing rounds all af-ter-noon,_____

Eat - ing at a greas - y spoon_____ To save on my

dough._____

At____ my ti - ny____ flat_____ There's just my____ cat,_____ A____ bed____

____ and a chair._____ Still____ I'll stick it____ till_____ I'm on a____ bill____

All ov - er Times Square. Some day, may-be,

If I stick it long e -nough I can get to strut my stuff,

Work - ing for a nice man Like a Zieg - field or a Weiss - man In a

great big Broad - way show!

ff

Cabaret
from the Musical CABARET

Words by Fred Ebb

Music by John Kander

Moderately

What good is sit - ting, a -
Put down the knit - ting, the

lone in your room? ___ Come hear the mu - sic
book and the broom, ___ time for a hol - i -

play; ___
day; ___

Life is a

cab - a - ret, old chum, _____

come to the cab - a - ret. _____

ret. Come taste the wine, come hear the

band, come blow the horn, start cel - e - brat - ing,

Can You Feel the Love Tonight

from Disney Presents THE LION KING: THE BROADWAY MUSICAL

Lyrics by Tim Rice

Music by Elton John

man - y things to tell her, but how to make her see the

truth a - bout my past. Im - pos - si - ble! She'd turn a - way from me. He's

hold - ing back. He's hid - ing. But what? I can't de - cide. Why

won't he be the king I know he is, the king I see in - side?

NALA:

Can't Help Lovin' Dat Man

from SHOW BOAT

Lyrics by Oscar Hammerstein II

Music by Jerome Kern

de an - gels done plan.

De chimb-ley's smok-in', de roof is leak-in' in, _____ but he don't _____

_____ seem to care. _____ He can be hap-py 'wid jus' a sip of

gin. _____ I e - ven loves him when _____

his kiss - es got gin. _____

Fish got to swim _ and birds got to fly, _ I got to love _ one

man till I die _ Can't help lov - in' dat man _ of

mine. _____ Tell me he's la - zy,

back dat day is fine, _____ de sun will shine.

He can come home __ as late as can be; ____ home wid-out him __ ain't

no home to me. __ Can't help lov-in' dat man __ of

mine.

mine. _____

Children Will Listen

from INTO THE WOODS

Words and Music by
Stephen Sondheim

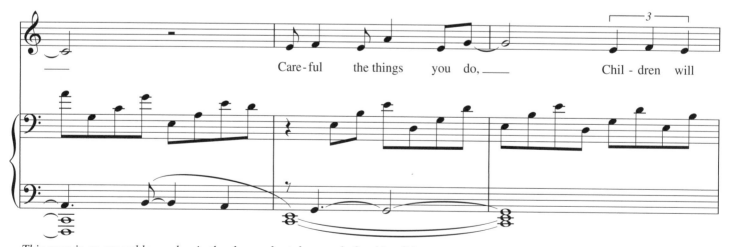

This song is an ensemble number in the show, adapted as a solo for this edition.

see.   And   learn.

cresc. poco a poco

mp

Chil-dren may not   o - bey, ___   But

mp

chil-dren will lis - ten. ___   Chil dren will look _ to you ___

For   which way   to   turn, ___   To

cresc.

learn what to be. _____ Care-ful be-fore ___ you say, ___

"Lis - ten to me." _____ Chil-dren will

lis - ten. _____ Care-ful the wish you make, _

Wish - es are chil - dren. _____

Care - ful the path they take — Wish - es come true,

Not free.

Care - ful the spell you cast, _

Not just on chil - dren. ____

cresc. poco a poco

mf

79

Some-times the spell _ may last _____ Past what you can see _____

And turn a-gainst you... _____

Care-ful the tale _ you tell. _____ *That* is the spell. _____

Chil-dren will lis-ten...

poco rit.

80

Circle of Life

from Disney Presents THE LION KING: THE BROADWAY MUSICAL

Lyrics by Tim Rice

Music by Elton John

RAFIKI & CHORUS:

It's the cir - cle of life

and it moves us all ___ through de - spair and

Comedy Tonight

from A FUNNY THING HAPPENED ON THE WAY TO THE FORUM

Words and Music by
Stephen Sondheim

Consider Yourself

from the Broadway Musical OLIVER!

Words and Music by
Lionel Bart

Don't Cry for Me Argentina

from EVITA

Words by Tim Rice

Music by Andrew Lloyd Webber

nines,   at six - es and sev - ens with you.

I had to let it hap - pen, I had to change,   could - n't spend all my life down at

heel,   look - ing out of the win - dow, stay - ing out of the sun.   So I chose

free - dom,   run - ning a - round try - ing ev - 'ry - thing new,   but noth - ing im - pressed me at all, _

And as for for - tune and as for fame, I

nev - er in - vit - ed them in, though it seemed to the world _ they were

all I de - sired. They are il - lu - sions, they're

not the so - lu - tions they prom - ised to be, the an - swer was here all the

ti - na, _____ the truth is I nev - er left you. All through my

wild days, _____ my mad ex - is - tence, I kept my prom - ise, don't keep your

dis - tance. _____ Have I said too much, there's noth - ing more I can think of to

say to you. ___ But all you have to do is

look at me to know that ev - 'ry word is true. __

Everything's Coming Up Roses

from GYPSY

Lyrics by Stephen Sondheim

Music by Jule Styne

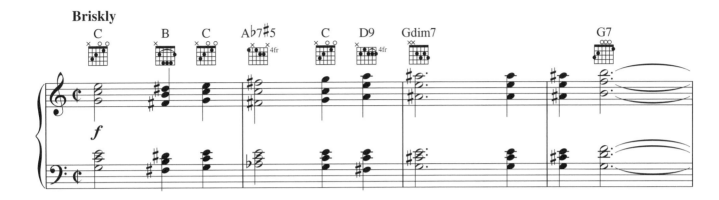

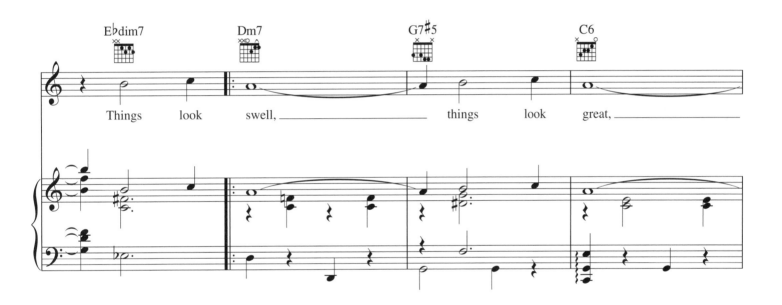

Things look swell, _____ things look great, _____

_____ gon - na have the whole world _____ on a plate. _____

Getting to Know You

from THE KING AND I

Lyrics by Oscar Hammerstein II

Music by Richard Rodgers

Godspeed Titanic

(Sail On)

from TITANIC

Music and Lyrics by
Maury Yeston

Hello, Dolly!

from HELLO, DOLLY!

Music and Lyric by
Jerry Herman

Hey There

from THE PAJAMA GAME

Words and Music by
Richard Adler and Jerry Ross

How Are Things in Glocca Morra

from FINIAN'S RAINBOW

Words by E.Y. "Yip" Harburg

Music by Burton Lane

breeze; _____ it well may be it's fol - lowed me a - cross the

seas. _____ Then tell me, please: _____ how are things in Gloc - ca

Moderately slow

Mor - ra? _____ Is that lit - tle brook still leap - ing there? _____

___ Does it still run down to Don - ny cove? _____ Through Kil - ly - begs, _____ Kil -

I Am What I Am
from LA CAGE AUX FOLLES

Music and Lyric by
Jerry Herman

am   needs ____ no   ex - cus - es. ____

____ I   deal ____ my   own

deck,   some - times   the   ace,   some -

- times   the   deuc - es. ____ { There's

It's

131

I Believe in You

from HOW TO SUCCEED IN BUSINESS WITHOUT REALLY TRYING

By Frank Loesser

I Can Hear the Bells

from HAIRSPRAY

Lyrics by
Marc Shaiman and Scott Wittman

Music by Marc Shaiman

Slowly and freely

I can — hear the bells. Well, don't cha — hear 'em chime?

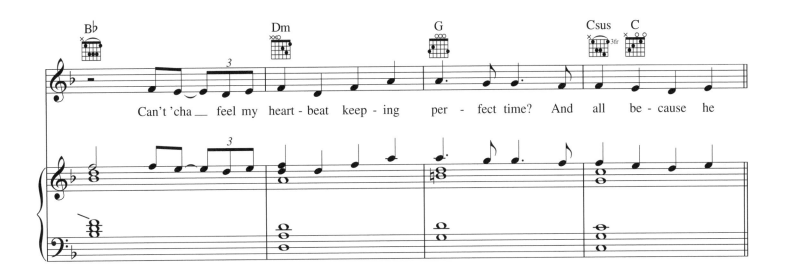

Can't 'cha — feel my heart-beat keep-ing per - fect time? And all be - cause he

Moderate Rock beat

touched me. He looked at ___ me and stared. Yes, he bumped me. My

knocked me out, and I can ___ hear the bells. My head is spin - ning.

I can ___ hear the bells. Some-thing's be - gin - ning. Ev - 'ry - bod - y says that a

girl who looks like me can't win his love. Well, just wait and see, 'cause

I can ___ hear the bells. Just hear them chim - ing. I can ___ hear the bells. My

tem-p'ra-ture's climb-ing. I can't con-tain my joy 'cause I fin-'ly___ found the boy I've been

miss-in'. Lis-ten! I can hear the be-ells.___

Round one, he'll ask me___ on a date, and then round two, I'll

walks me down the aisle. _____ My moth-er starts to cry, but I can't see 'cause Link and I are French-

kiss - in'. Lis - ten! I can _____ hear the bells. _____

I can _____ hear the bells. My head is reel - in'. I can _____ hear the bells. I

I Enjoy Being a Girl

from FLOWER DRUM SONG

Lyrics by Oscar Hammerstein II

Music by Richard Rodgers

gait _____ With my hips kind of swiv-el-ly and

swerv-y. _____ I a - dore be-ing dressed in some-thing

fril-ly _____ When my date comes to get me at my place. Out I

go with my Joe or John or Bill-y, _____ Like a fil-ly who is

read - y   for the   race! _____   When

Refrain (brightly)

I   have   a   brand - new   hair - do _____   With   my

eye - lash - es   all   in   curl, _____   I

float   as   the   clouds   on   air   do, _____   I   en -

joy be - ing a girl! _____

When men say I'm cute and

fun - ny _____ And my teeth are - n't

teeth but pearl, _____ I

149

just lap it up like hon - ey _____ I en -
joy be - ing a girl! _____
I flip when a fel - low sends me
flow - ers, _____ I drool o - ver

If I Loved You

from CAROUSEL

Lyrics by Oscar Hammerstein II

Music by Richard Rodgers

If I loved you, Words ____ would-n't come ___ in an eas - y way, 'Round in cir - cles I'd go. _____ Long - in' to tell you, but a - fraid and shy, I'd let my gold - en chanc - es pass me

by!   Soon   you'd   leave   me,   off ___ you would go ___ in the

mist   of   day,   Nev -   er,   nev - er   to   know ___

How   I   loved you,   If   I

mf molto espr.   *f*   *rit.*

loved   you.   loved   you. ___

a tempo

L.H.

157

If I Were a Bell

from GUYS AND DOLLS

By Frank Loesser

were a gate ___ I'd be swing - ing. _____ And if
___ I'd be splash - ing my dress - ing. _____ Or if

I were a watch I'd start pop - ping my spring, _____
I were a sea - son I'd sure - ly be Spring, _____

___ or if I were a bell ___ I'd go ding dong ding dong
___ or if I were a bell ___ I'd go ding dong ding dong

ding. Ask me ding. _____

If My Friends Could See Me Now

from SWEET CHARITY

Lyrics by Dorothy Fields

Music by Cy Coleman

What a set - up!
What a build - up!
What a step up! Ho - ly cow! They'd nev-er be - lieve it, if my

friends could see me now!

If they could friends could see

me now!

The Impossible Dream
(The Quest)
from MAN OF LA MANCHA

Lyric by Joe Darion

Music by Mitch Leigh

right _____ with-out ques-tion or pause, _____ to be will-ing to

march in-to hell for a heav en-ly cause! And I know, _____ if I'll on-ly be

true _____ to this glo-ri-ous quest, _____ that my

heart _____ will lie peace-ful and calm, _____ when I'm laid to my

It's De-Lovely

from RED, HOT AND BLUE!

Words and Music by
Cole Porter

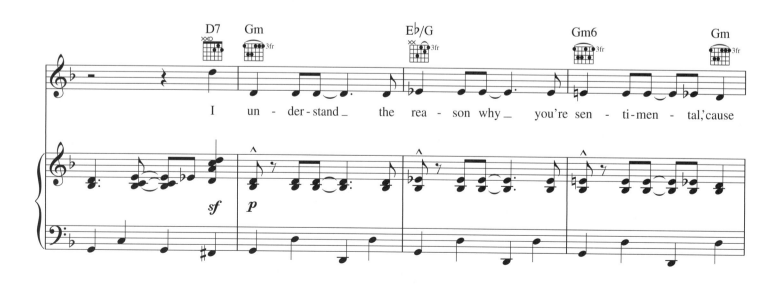

Mack the Knife
from THE THREEPENNY OPERA

English Words by Marc Blitzstein
Original German Words by Bert Brecht

Music by Kurt Weill

sight. _____ When the shark bites _____ with his teeth, dear, _____

_____ scar - let bil - lows _____ start to spread. _____ Fan - cy

gloves, though, _____ wears Mac - heath, dear, _____ so there's

not a _____ trace of red. _____ On the

Mame

from MAME

Music and Lyric by
Jerry Herman

Lyrics:

You coax the blues right out ___ of the horn, Mame, ___
You've brought the cake-walk back ___ in-to style, Mame, ___

you charm the husk right off ___ of the corn, Mame. ___
you make the weep-in' wil-low tree smile, Mame. ___

You've got the ban-joes strum-min' and plunk-in' out a tune to beat the
Your skin is Dix-ie sat-in, there's reb-el in your man-ner and your

Man of La Mancha
(I, Don Quixote)
from MAN OF LA MANCHA

Lyric by Joe Darion

Music by Mitch Leigh

My Favorite Things

from THE SOUND OF MUSIC

Lyrics by Oscar Hammerstein II

Music by Richard Rodgers

New York, New York

from ON THE TOWN

Lyrics by
Betty Comden and Adolph Green

Music by Leonard Bernstein

Lyrics (verse):

We've got one day here, and not an-oth-er
min-ute to see the fa-mous sights;

The fa-mous plac-es to vis-it are so
man-y, or so the guide-books say;

Man-hat-tan wom-en are dressed in silk and
sat-in, or so the fel-lows say;

York, New York, _____

it's a hell - uv - a town! _____

Not While I'm Around

from SWEENEY TODD

Words and Music by
Stephen Sondheim

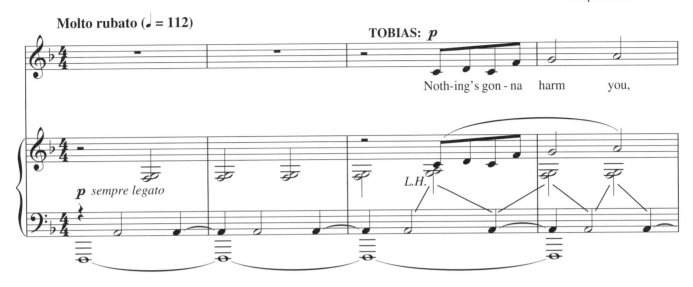

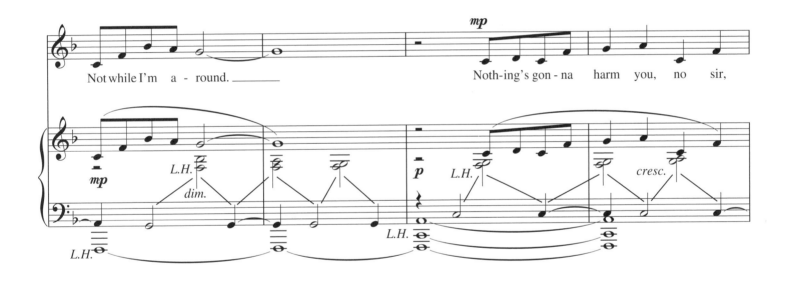

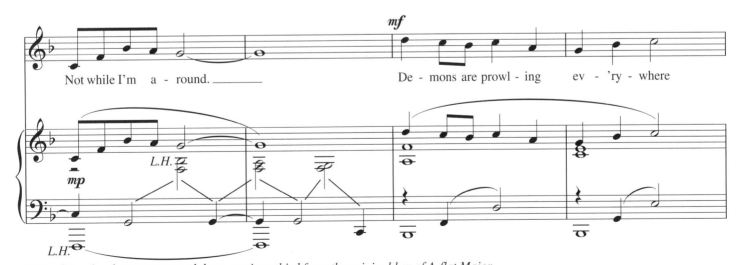

This edition has been transposed down a minor third from the original key of A-flat Major.

now - a - days. _____ I'll send 'em howl - ing, I don't care...

I got ways. _____

No one's gon - na hurt you, No one's gon - na dare. _____

Oth - ers can de - sert you, Not to wor - ry, Whis - tle, I'll be there. _____

Show me some-thing I can o - ver - come. Not to wor - ry,

mum.

Be - ing close and be - ing clev - er ain't like be - ing

true.

I don't need to, I won't nev - er hide a thing from

you, Like some.

No one's gon - na

hurt you, No one's gon - na dare. _____ Oth - ers can de -

sert you, Not to wor - ry, Whis tle, I'll be there. _____ De - mons 'll charm you

with a smile For a while, But in time Noth - ing's gon - na harm you,

Not while I'm a - round. _____

Oh, What a Beautiful Mornin'

from OKLAHOMA!

Lyrics by Oscar Hammerstein II

Music by Richard Rodgers

Moderate Waltz

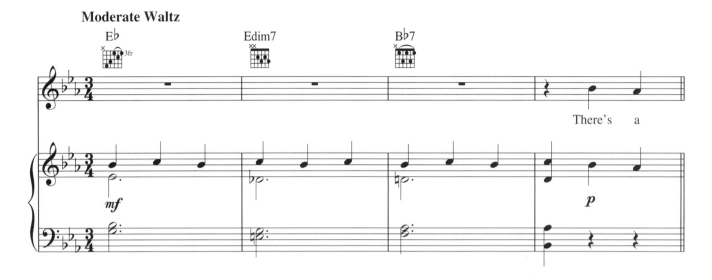

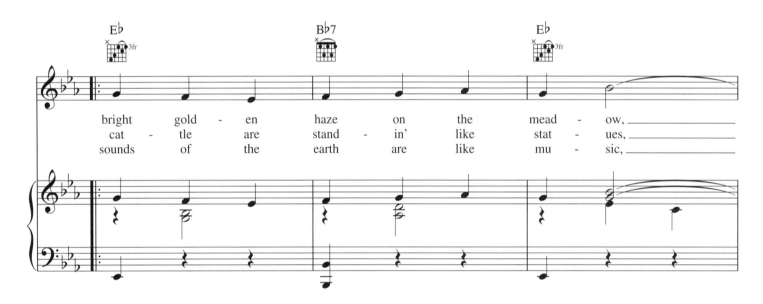

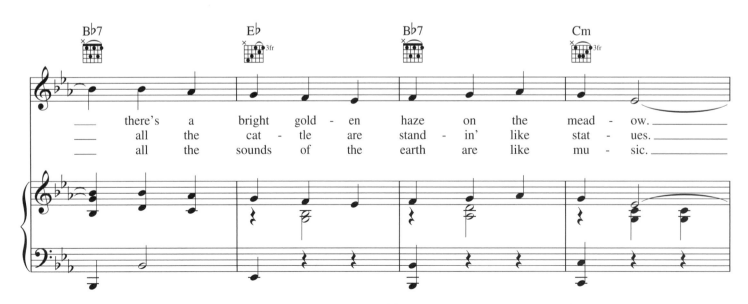

The corn is as high as an el-e-phant's
They don't turn as their heads as they see me ride
The breeze is so bus-y it don't miss a

eye, an' it looks like it's climb-in' clear
by, but a lit-tle brown mav'-rick is
tree, and a ol' weep-in' wil-ler is

up to the sky.
wink-in' her eye.
laugh-in' at me!

Oh, what a beau-ti-ful

morn-in'. Oh, what a beau-ti-ful

On My Own

from LES MISÉRABLES

Lyrics by
Alain Boublil, Jean-Marc Natel,
Herbert Kretzmer, John Caird
and Trevor Nunn

Music by Claude-Michel Schönberg

out me his world will go on turn - ing. _____ The world is full of hap-pi-ness that I have nev-er known. I love him, _____ I love him, _____ I love him, _____ but on-ly on my own.

Part of Your World

from Walt Disney's THE LITTLE MERMAID - A BROADWAY MUSICAL

Lyrics by Howard Ashman

Music by Alan Menken

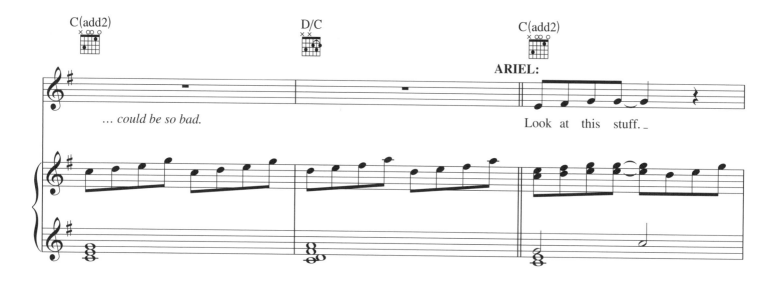

207

plore that shore up a - bove? _____ Out of the

sea, wish I could be

part of that world. _____

Popular

from the Broadway Musical WICKED

Music and Lyrics by
Stephen Schwartz

prop - er ploys __ when you talk to boys, __ lit - tle ways to flirt and flounce __

__ I'll show you what shoes to wear, how to fix your hair, __

ev - 'ry - thing that real - ly counts __ to be pop - u - lar! __ I'll help __ you be

pop - u - lar! You'll hang __ with the right co - horts, __ you'll be

staccato

212

good at sports,__ know the slang you've got to know __ So let's

start, 'cause you've got an aw-f'lly long__ way to go! _____

Don't be of-fend-ed by my frank an - al - y - sis Think of it as per-son-al-i-

chugging along

ty di-al - y-sis Now that I've cho-sen to be - come a pal,__ a sis-

Put On a Happy Face

from BYE BYE BIRDIE

Lyrics by Lee Adams

Music by Charles Strouse

221

Seasons of Love

from RENT

Words and Music by
Jonathan Larson

day-lights, in sun-sets, in mid-nights, in cups __ of cof-fee, in inch - es, in miles, in

laugh-ter, in ___ strife, __ in five hun-dred twen-ty-five thou-sand six hun-dred min - utes. How

do you meas-ure a year in __ the life? __ How a-bout love? _____

_____ How a-bout love? _____ How a-bout

Someone Like You

from the Broadway Musical JEKYLL & HYDE

Words by Leslie Bricusse

Music by Frank Wildhorn

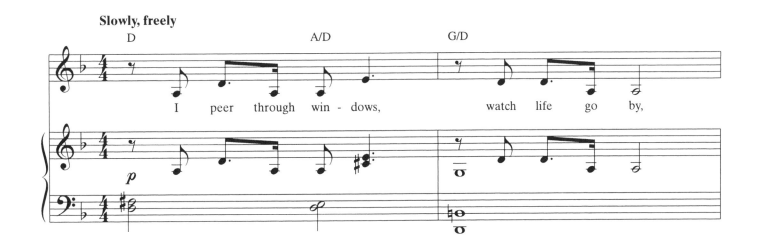

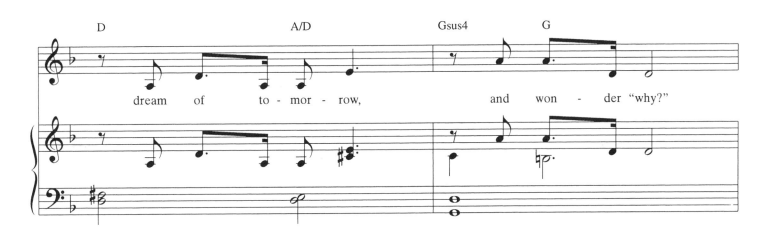

feel so a - live,_____ if some - one like you_____ found
me! So man - y se - crets
I long to share! All I have need - ed
is some - one there to help me see a world

Sunrise, Sunset

from the Musical FIDDLER ON THE ROOF

Words by Sheldon Harnick

Music by Jerry Bock

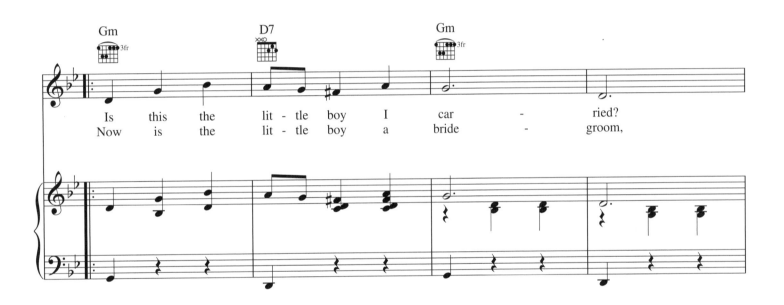

Is this the lit - tle boy I car - ried?
Now is the lit - tle boy a bride - groom,

Is this the lit - tle girl at play?
now is the lit - tle girl a bride?

I don't re -
Un - der the

234

There's a Fine, Fine Line

from AVENUE Q

Music and Lyrics by
Robert Lopez and Jeff Marx

fine, fine line _____ be-tween to - geth - er and not.

And there's a fine, fine line _____ be-tween what you

want - ed and what you got. You

got - ta go af - ter the things _____ you want _ while you're _ still _ in _____ your prime... _

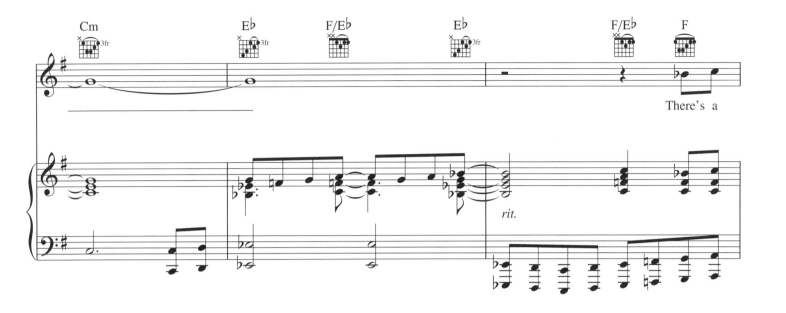

Broader

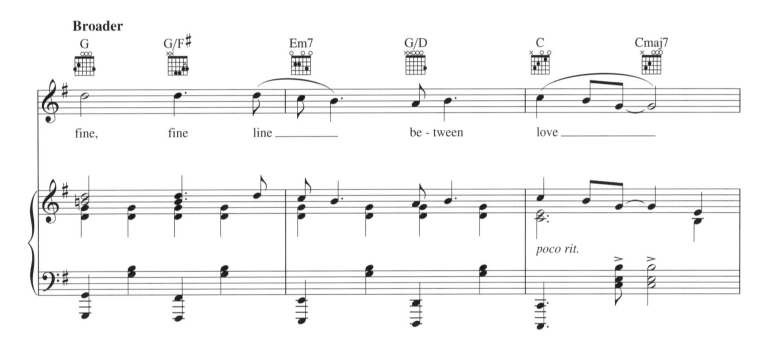

fine, fine line _____ be - tween love _____

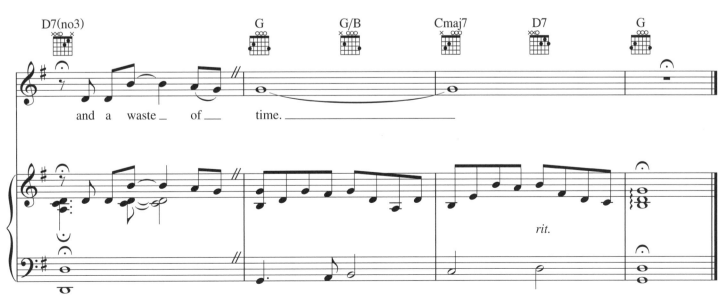

and a waste _ of _ time. _____

There's No Business Like Show Business

from the Stage Production ANNIE GET YOUR GUN

Words and Music by
Irving Berlin

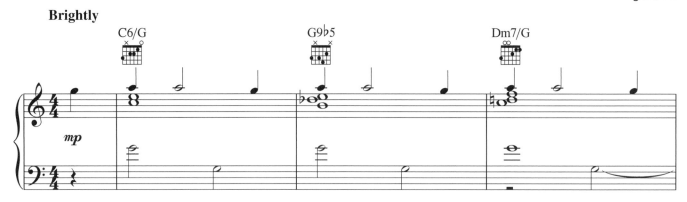

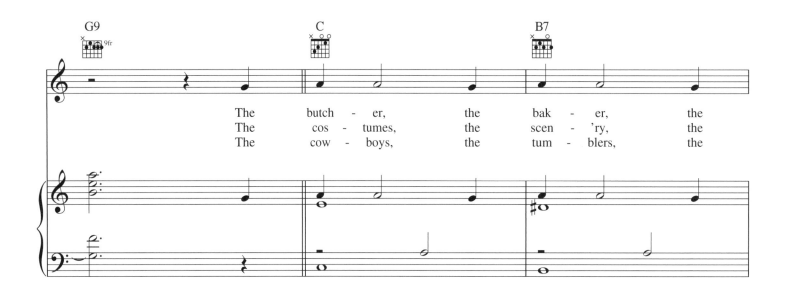

The butch - er, the bak - er, the
The cos - tumes, the scen - 'ry, the
The cow - boys, the tum - blers, the

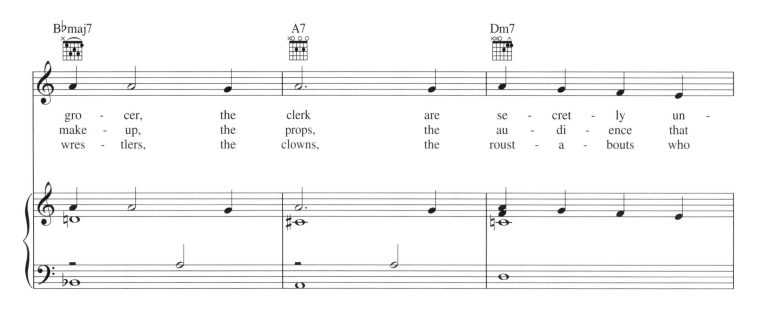

gro - cer, the clerk are se - cret - ly un -
make - up, the props, the au - di - ence that
wres - tlers, the clowns, the roust - a - bouts who

an-y-thing the-a-tri-cal and why._____ There's
clos-ing when the cus-tom-ers won't come._____ There's
towel you've tak-en from the last ho-tel._____ There's

rit.   *a tempo*

no bus'-ness like show bus'-ness like
no bus'-ness like show bus'-ness like
no bus'-ness like show bus'-ness like

no bus'-ness I know._____
no bus'-ness I know._____
no bus'-ness I know._____

Ev-'ry-thing a-bout it is ap-peal-ing._____
You get word be-fore the show has start-ed._____
Trav-'ling through the coun-try will be thrill-ing._____

This Is the Moment

from JEKYLL & HYDE

Words by Leslie Bricusse

Music by Frank Wildhorn

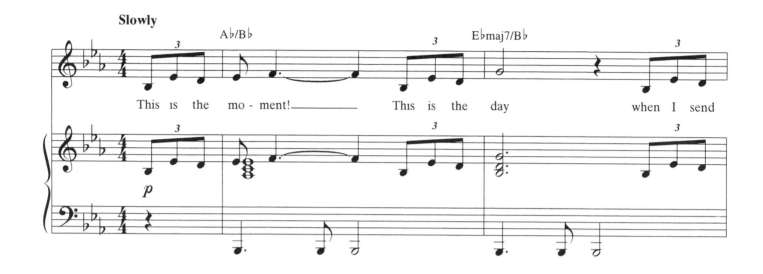

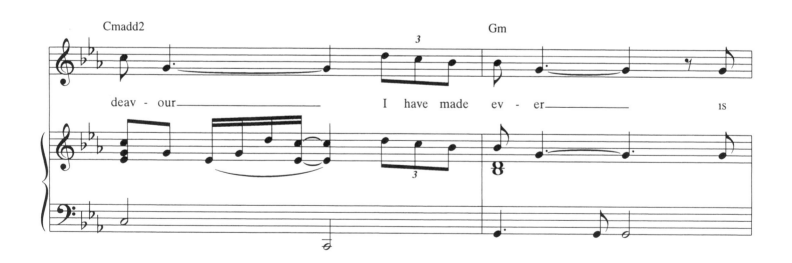

252

Till There Was You

from Meredith Willson's THE MUSIC MAN

By Meredith Willson

Moderately

There were bells on the hill, but I never heard them ring-ing. No, I never heard them at all till there was you.

There were

Tomorrow
from the Musical Production ANNIE

Lyric by Martin Charnin

Music by Charles Strouse

clears a - way the cob - webs and the sor - row _____ till there's

none. When I'm stuck ___ with a day that's gray and

lone - ly, I just stick ___ out my chin and grin and

say: _____ Oh! the

Under the Sea

from Walt Disney's THE LITTLE MERMAID - A BROADWAY MUSICAL

Lyrics by Howard Ashman

Music by Alan Menken

add WOMEN (bottom):

play the bass, and they ___ sound - in' sharp. The bass ___ play the brass, the chub ___

play the bass, and they ___ sound - in' sharp. The bass ___ play the brass, the chub ___

___ play the tub. The fluke is the duke of soul. The ray, ___

___ play the tub. The fluke is the duke of soul. The ray, ___

___ he can play. The ling's ___ on the strings. The trout ___ rock - in' out. The black-

___ he can play. The ling's ___ on the strings. The trout ___ rock - in' out. The black-

cresc. poco a poco

Unusual Way

from NINE

Music and Lyrics by
Maury Yeston

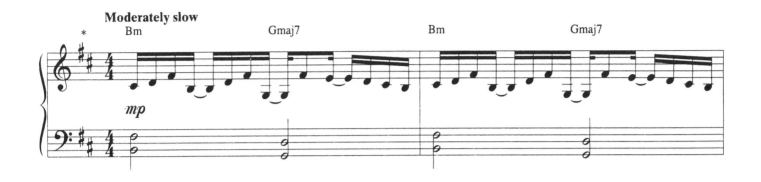

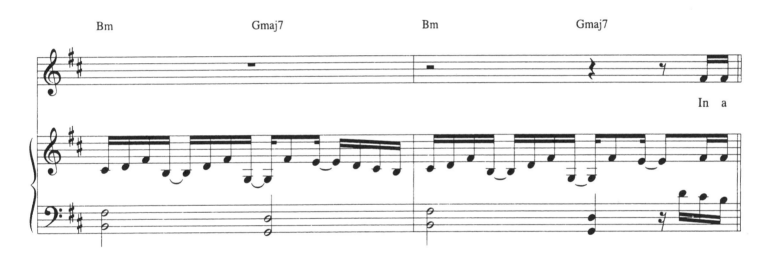

ver-y un-u-su-al way—— one time I need-ed you. In a
ver-y un-u-su-al way—— I think I'm in love with you. In a

* Recorded a half step lower.

ver - y un - u - su - al way___ you were my friend.
ver - y un - u - su - al way___ I want to cry.

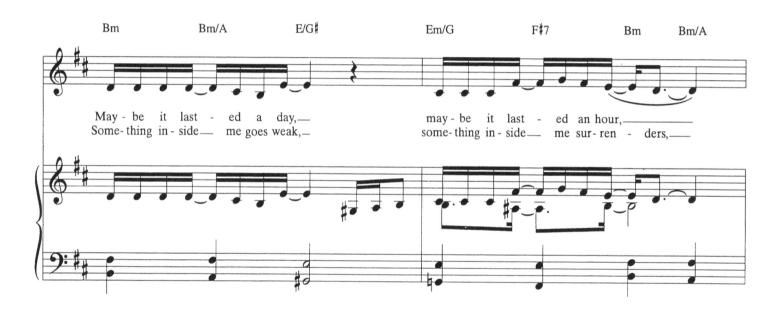

May - be it last - ed a day,___ may - be it last - ed an hour,___
Some - thing in - side___ me goes weak,___ some - thing in - side___ me sur - ren - ders,___

but some - how it will nev - er end.___ In a

and you're the rea - son why___   you're the rea - son

why.   You don't___ know___ what you do to me;

you don't___ have a clue.___   You can't___ tell___ what it's like to be

me,   look-ing at   you.   It scares me so___ that I can hard - ly

279

What I Did for Love

from A CHORUS LINE

Lyric by Edward Kleban

Music by Marvin Hamlisch

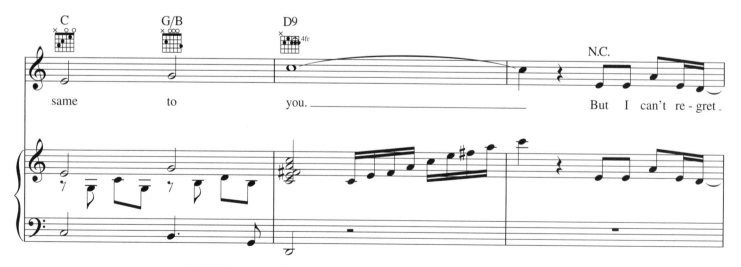

What Kind of Fool Am I?

from the Musical Production STOP THE WORLD—I WANT TO GET OFF

Words and Music by
Leslie Bricusse and Anthony Newley

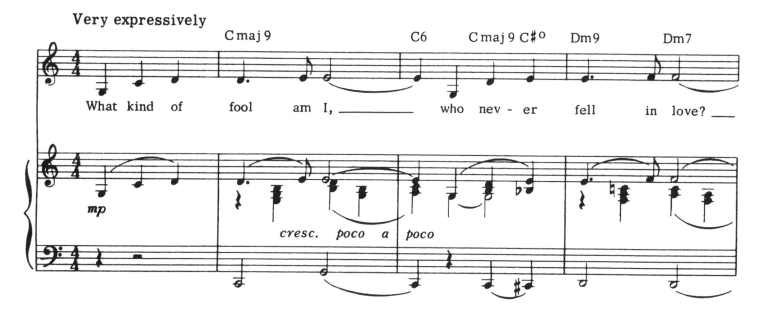

A Wonderful Guy

from SOUTH PACIFIC

Lyrics by Oscar Hammerstein II

Music by Richard Rodgers

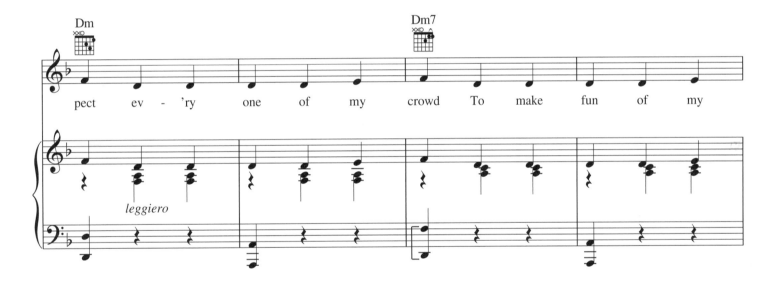

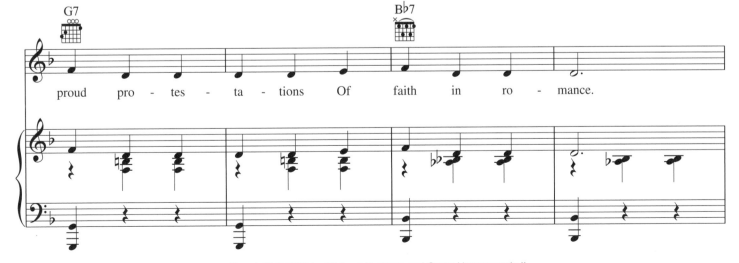

And you will note there's a lump in my throat When I speak of that won - der - ful guy! I'm as trite and as gay as a dai - sy in May, A cli - ché com - ing true!

You Walk with Me

from THE FULL MONTY

Words and Music by
David Yazbek

*Sing the top line melody in this section for a solo version of the song.

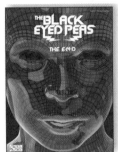

More Big-Note & Easy Piano Books

For a complete listing of Cherry Lane titles available, including contents listings, please visit our web site at www.cherrylane.

CHOPIN FOR EASY PIANO

This special easy piano version features the composer's intricate melodies, harmonies and rhythms newly arranged so that virtually all pianists can experience the thrill of playing Chopin at the piano! Includes 20 favorites mazurkas, nocturnes, polonaises, preludes and waltzes.
_____02501483 Easy Piano...............$7.99

CLASSICAL CHRISTMAS

Easy solo arrangements of 30 wonderful holiday songs: Ave Maria • Dance of the Sugar Plum Fairy • Evening Prayer • Gesu Bambino • Hallelujah! • He Shall Feed His Flock • March of the Toys • O Come, All Ye Faithful • O Holy Night • Pastoral Symphony • Sheep May Safely Graze • Sinfonia • Waltz of the Flowers • and more.
_____02500112 Easy Piano Solo.......$9.95

BEST OF JOHN DENVER

A collection of 18 Denver classics, including: Leaving on a Jet Plane • Take Me Home, Country Roads • Rocky Mountain High • Follow Me • and more.
_____02505512 Easy Piano...............$9.95

JOHN DENVER ANTHOLOGY

Easy arrangements of 34 of the finest from this beloved artist. Includes: Annie's Song • Fly Away • Follow Me • Grandma's Feather Bed • Leaving on a Jet Plane • Perhaps Love • Rocky Mountain High • Sunshine on My Shoulders • Take Me Home, Country Roads • Thank God I'm a Country Boy • and many more.
_____02501366 Easy Piano............$19.99

EASY BROADWAY SHOWSTOPPERS

Easy piano arrangements of 16 traditional and new Broadway standards, including: "Impossible Dream" from *Man of La Mancha* • "Unusual Way" from *Nine* • "This Is the Moment" from *Jekyll & Hyde* • many more.
_____02505517 Easy Piano............$12.95

A FAMILY CHRISTMAS AROUND THE PIANO

25 songs for hours of family fun, including: Away in a Manger • Deck the Hall • The First Noel • God Rest Ye Merry, Gentlemen • Hark! the Herald Angels Sing • Jingle Bells • Jolly Old St. Nicholas • Joy to the World • O Little Town of Bethlehem • Silent Night, Holy Night • The Twelve Days of Christmas • and more.
_____02500398 Easy Piano...............$8.99

FAVORITE CELTIC SONGS FOR EASY PIANO

Easy arrangements of 40 Celtic classics, including: The Ash Grove • The Bluebells of Scotland • A Bunch of Thyme • Danny Boy • Finnegan's Wake • I'll Tell Me Ma • Loch Lomond • My Wild Irish Rose • The Rose of Tralee • and more!
_____02501306 Easy Piano............$12.99

FAVORITE POP BALLADS

This new collection features 35 beloved ballads, including: Breathe (2 AM) • Faithfully • Leaving on a Jet Plane • Open Arms • Ordinary People • Summer Breeze • These Eyes • Truly • You've Got a Friend • and more.
_____02501005 Easy Piano............$15.99

HOLY CHRISTMAS CAROLS COLORING BOOK

A terrific songbook with 7 sacred carols and lots of coloring pages for the young pianist. Songs include: Angels We Have Heard on High • The First Noel • Hark! The Herald Angels Sing • It Came upon a Midnight Clear • O Come All Ye Faithful • O Little Town of Bethlehem • Silent Night.
_____02500277 Five-Finger Piano $6.95

JEKYLL & HYDE – VOCAL SELECTIONS

Ten songs from the Wildhorn/Bricusse Broadway smash, arranged for big-note: In His Eyes • It's a Dangerous Game • Lost in the Darkness • A New Life • No One Knows Who I Am • Once Upon a Dream • Someone Like You • Sympathy, Tenderness • Take Me as I Am • This Is the Moment.
_____02500023 Big-Note Piano........$9.95

JACK JOHNSON ANTHOLOGY

Easy arrangements of 27 of the best from this Hawaiian singer/songwriter, including: Better Together • Breakdown • Flake • Fortunate Fool • Good People • Sitting, Waiting, Wishing • Taylor • and more.
_____02501313 Easy Piano............$19.99

JUST FOR KIDS – NOT! CHRISTMAS SONGS

This unique collection of 14 Christmas favorites is fun for the whole family! Kids can play the full-sounding big-note solos alone, or with their parents (or teachers) playing accompaniment for the thrill of four-hand piano! Includes: Deck the Halls • Jingle Bells • Silent Night • What Child Is This? • and more.
_____02505510 Big-Note Piano........$8.95

JUST FOR KIDS – NOT! CLASSICS

Features big-note arrangements of classical masterpieces, plus optional accompaniment for adults. Songs: Air on the G String • Dance of the Sugar Plum Fairy • Für Elise • Jesu, Joy of Man's Desiring • Ode to Joy • Pomp and Circumstance • The Sorcerer's Apprentice • William Tell Overture • and more!
_____02505513 Classics $7.95
_____02500301 More Classics..........$8.95

JUST FOR KIDS – NOT! FUN SONGS

Fun favorites for kids everywhere in big-note arrangements for piano, including: Bingo • Eensy Weensy Spider • Farmer in the Dell • Jingle Bells • London Bridge • Pop Goes the Weasel • Puff the Magic Dragon • Skip to My Lou • Twinkle, Twinkle Little Star • and more!
_____02505523 Fun Songs $7.95

JUST FOR KIDS – NOT! TV THEMES & MOVIE SONGS

Entice the kids to the piano with this delightful collection of songs and themes from movies and TV. These big-note arrangements include themes from The Brady Bunch and The Addams Family, as well as Do-Re-Mi (The Sound of Music), theme from Beetlejuice (Day-O) and Puff the Magic Dragon. Each song includes an accompaniment part for teacher or adult so that the kids can experience the joy of four-hand playing as well! Plus performance tips.
_____02505507 TV Themes & Movie Songs.....................$9.95
_____02500304 More TV Themes & Movie Songs.....................$9.95

MERRY CHRISTMAS, EVERYONE

Over 20 contemporary and classic all-time holiday favorites arranged for big-note piano or easy piano. Includes: Away in a Manger • Christmas Like a Lullaby • The First Noel • Joy to the World • The Marvelous Toy • and more.
_____02505600 Big-Note Piano........$9.95

POKEMON 2 B.A. MASTER

This great songbook features easy piano arrangements of 13 tunes from the hit TV series: 2.B.A. Master • Double Trouble (Team Rocket) • Everything Changes • Misty's Song • My Best Friends • Pokémon (Dance Mix) • Pokémon Theme • PokéRAP • The Time Has Come (Pikachu's Goodbye) • Together, Forever • Viridian City • What Kind of Pokémon Are You? • You Can Do It (If You Really Try). Includes a full-color, 8-page pull-out section featuring characters and scenes from this super hot show.
_____02500145 Easy Piano............$12.95

POP/ROCK LOVE SONGS

Easy arrangements of 18 romatic favorites, including: Always • Bed of Roses • Butterfly Kisses • Follow Me • From This Moment On • Hard Habit to Break • Leaving on a Jet Plane • When You Say Nothing at All • more.
_____02500151 Easy Piano............$10.95

POPULAR CHRISTMAS CAROLS COLORING BOOK

Kids are sure to love this fun holiday songbook! It features five-finger piano arrangements of seven Christmas classics, complete with coloring pages throughout! Songs include: Deck the Hall • Good King Wenceslas • Jingle Bells • Jolly Old St. Nicholas • O Christmas Tree • Up on the Housetop • We Wish You a Merry Christmas.
_____02500276 Five-Finger Piano $6.95

PUFF THE MAGIC DRAGON & 54 OTHER ALL-TIME CHILDREN'S FAVORITESONGS

55 timeless songs enjoyed by generations of kids, and sure to be favorites for years to come. Songs include: A-Tisket A-Tasket • Alouette • Eensy Weensy Spider • The Farmer in the Dell • I've Been Working on the Railroad • If You're Happy and You Know It • Joy to the World • Michael Finnegan • Oh Where, Oh Where Has My Little Dog Gone • Silent Night • Skip to My Lou • This Old Man • and many more.
_____02500017 Big-Note Piano......$12.95

See your local music dealer or contact:

cherry lane music company

EXCLUSIVELY DISTRIBUTED BY
HAL•LEONARD®
7777 W. BLUEMOUND RD. P.O. BOX 13819 MILWAUKEE, WI 53213

Prices, contents, and availability subject to change without notice.

0811